Layers of Learning

Year Three • Unit Seventeen

Boston Tea Party
Japan
More Reactions
Folk Music

Published by HooDoo Publishing
United States of America
© 2015 Layers of Learning
Copies of maps or activities may be made for a particular family or classroom.

If you wish to reproduce or print excerpts of this publication, please contact us at contact@layers-of-learning.com for permission. Thank you for respecting copyright laws.

Units At A Glance: Topics For All Four Years of the Layers of Learning Program

1	History	Geography	Science	The Arts
1	Mesopotamia	Maps & Globes	Planets	Cave Paintings
2	Egypt	Map Keys	Stars	Egyptian Art
3	Europe	Global Grids	Earth & Moon	Crafts
4	Ancient Greece	Wonders	Satellites	Greek Art
5	Babylon	Mapping People	Humans in Space	Poetry
6	The Levant	Physical Earth	Laws of Motion	List Poems
7	Phoenicians	Oceans	Motion	Moral Stories
8	Assyrians	Deserts	Fluids	Rhythm
9	Persians	Arctic	Waves	Melody
10	Ancient China	Forests	Machines	Chinese Art
11	Early Japan	Mountains	States of Matter	Line & Shape
12	Arabia	Rivers & Lakes	Atoms	Color & Value
13	Ancient India	Grasslands	Elements	Texture & Form
14	Ancient Africa	Africa	Bonding	African Tales
15	First North Americans	North America	Salts	Creative Kids
16	Ancient South America	South America	Plants	South American Art
17	Celts	Europe	Flowering Plants	Jewelry
18	Roman Republic	Asia	Trees	Roman Art
19	Christianity	Australia & Oceania	Simple Plants	Instruments
20	Roman Empire	You Explore	Fungi	Composing Music

2	History	Geography	Science	The Arts
1	Byzantines	Turkey	Climate & Seasons	Byzantine Art
2	Barbarians	Ireland	Forecasting	Illumination
3	Islam	Arabian Peninsula	Clouds & Precipitation	Creative Kids
4	Vikings	Norway	Special Effects	Viking Art
5	Anglo Saxons	Britain	Wild Weather	King Arthur Tales
6	Charlemagne	France	Cells and DNA	Carolingian Art
7	Normans	Nigeria	Skeletons	Canterbury Tales
8	Feudal System	Germany	Muscles, Skin, & Cardiopulmonary	Gothic Art
9	Crusades	Balkans	Digestive & Senses	Religious Art
10	Burgundy, Venice, Spain	Switzerland	Nerves	Oil Paints
11	Wars of the Roses	Russia	Health	Minstrels & Plays
12	Eastern Europe	Hungary	Metals	Printmaking
13	African Kingdoms	Mali	Carbon Chem	Textiles
14	Asian Kingdoms	Southeast Asia	Non-metals	Vivid Language
15	Mongols	Caucasus	Gases	Fun With Poetry
16	Medieval China & Japan	China	Electricity	Asian Arts
17	Pacific Peoples	Micronesia	Circuits	Arts of the Islands
18	American Peoples	Canada	Technology	Indian Legends
19	The Renaissance	Italy	Magnetism	Renaissance Art I
20	Explorers	Caribbean Sea	Motors	Renaissance Art II

3	History	Geography	Science	The Arts
1	Age of Exploration	Argentina and Chile	Classification & Insects	Fairy Tales
2	The Ottoman Empire	Egypt and Libya	Reptiles & Amphibians	Poetry
3	Mogul Empire	Pakistan & Afghanistan	Fish	Mogul Arts
4	Reformation	Angola & Zambia	Birds	Reformation Art
5	Renaissance England	Tanzania & Kenya	Mammals & Primates	Shakespeare
6	Thirty Years' War	Spain	Sound	Baroque Music
7	The Dutch	Netherlands	Light & Optics	Baroque Art I
8	France	Indonesia	Bending Light	Baroque Art II
9	The Enlightenment	Korean Pen.	Color	Art Journaling
10	Russia & Prussia	Central Asia	History of Science	Watercolors
11	Conquistadors	Baltic States	Igneous Rocks	Creative Kids
12	Settlers	Peru & Bolivia	Sedimentary Rocks	Native American Art
13	13 Colonies	Central America	Metamorphic Rocks	Settler Sayings
14	Slave Trade	Brazil	Gems & Minerals	Colonial Art
15	The South Pacific	Australasia	Fossils	Principles of Art
16	The British in India	India	Chemical Reactions	Classical Music
17	Boston Tea Party	Japan	Reversible Reactions	Folk Music
18	Founding Fathers	Iran	Compounds & Solutions	Rococo
19	Declaring Independence	Samoa and Tonga	Oxidation & Reduction	Creative Crafts I
20	The American Revolution	South Africa	Acids & Bases	Creative Crafts II

4	History	Geography	Science	The Arts
1	American Government	USA	Heat & Temperature	Patriotic Music
2	Expanding Nation	Pacific States	Motors & Engines	Tall Tales
3	Industrial Revolution	U.S. Landscapes	Energy	Romantic Art I
4	Revolutions	Mountain West States	Energy Sources	Romantic Art II
5	Africa	U.S. Political Maps	Energy Conversion	Impressionism I
6	The West	Southwest States	Earth Structure	Impressionism II
7	Civil War	National Parks	Plate Tectonics	Post-Impressionism
8	World War I	Plains States	Earthquakes	Expressionism
9	Totalitarianism	U.S. Economics	Volcanoes	Abstract Art
10	Great Depression	Heartland States	Mountain Building	Kinds of Art
11	World War II	Symbols and Landmarks	Chemistry of Air & Water	War Art
12	Modern East Asia	The South States	Food Chemistry	Modern Art
13	India's Independence	People of America	Industry	Pop Art
14	Israel	Appalachian States	Chemistry of Farming	Modern Music
15	Cold War	U.S. Territories	Chemistry of Medicine	Free Verse
16	Vietnam War	Atlantic States	Food Chains	Photography
17	Latin America	New England States	Animal Groups	Latin American Art
18	Civil Rights	Home State Study	Instincts	Theater & Film
19	Technology	Home State Study II	Habitats	Architecture
20	Terrorism	America in Review	Conservation	Creative Kids

This unit includes printables at the end. To make life easier for you we also created digital printable packs for each unit. To retrieve your printable pack for Unit 3-17, please visit

www.layers-of-learning.com/digital-printable-packs/

Put the printable pack in your shopping cart and use this coupon code:

0810UNIT3-17

Your printable pack will be free.

LAYERS OF LEARNING INTRODUCTION

This is part of a series of units in the Layers of Learning homeschool curriculum, including the subjects of history, geography, science, and the arts. Children from 1st through 12th can participate in the same curriculum at the same time - family school style.

The units are intended to be used in order as the basis of a complete curriculum (once you add in a systematic math, reading, and writing program). You begin with Year 1 Unit 1 no matter what ages your children are. Spend about 2 weeks on each unit. You pick and choose the activities within the unit that appeal to you and read the books from the book list that are available to you or find others on the same topic from your library. We highly recommend that you use the timeline in every history section as the backbone. Then flesh out your learning with reading and activities that highlight the topics you think are the most important.

Alternatively, you can use the units as activity ideas to supplement another curriculum in any order you wish. You can still use them with all ages of children at the same time.

When you've finished with Year One, move on to Year Two, Year Three, and Year Four. Then begin again with Year One and work your way through the years again. Now your children will be older, reading more involved books, and writing more in depth. When you have completed the sequence for the second time, you start again on it for the third and final time. If your student began with Layers of Learning in 1st grade and stayed with it all the way through she would go through the four year rotation three times, firmly cementing the information in her mind in ever increasing depth. At each level you should expect increasing amounts of outside reading and writing. High schoolers in particular should be reading extensively, and if possible, participating in discussion groups.

☺ ☺ ☺ These icons will guide you in spotting activities and books that are appropriate for the age of child you are working with. But if you think an activity is too juvenile or too difficult for your kids, adjust accordingly. The icons are not there as rules, just guides.

☺ GRADES 1-4
☺ GRADES 5-8
☺ GRADES 9-12

Within each unit we share:
- EXPLORATIONS, activities relating to the topic;
- EXPERIMENTS, usually associated with science topics;
- EXPEDITIONS, field trips;
- EXPLANATIONS, teacher helps or educational philosophies.

In the sidebars we also include Additional Layers, Famous Folks, Fabulous Facts, On the Web, and other extra related topics that can take you off on tangents, exploring the world and your interests with a bit more freedom. The curriculum will always be there to pull you back on track when you're ready.

You can learn more about how to use this curriculum at www.layers-of-learning.com/layers-of-learning-program/.

BOSTON TEA PARTY – JAPAN – MORE REACTIONS – FOLK MUSIC

UNIT SEVENTEEN
BOSTON TEA PARTY – JAPAN – MORE REACTIONS – FOLK MUSIC

Free people, remember this maxim: May we acquire liberty, but it is never recovered if it is once lost.
-Jean Jacques Rousseau

LIBRARY LIST:

Search for: Boston Tea Party, French and Indian War, Samuel Adams, Sons of Liberty

- Boston Tea Party by Pamela Duncan Edwards. A picture book uses mice to tell the story of the Boston Tea Party in sing-song cadence.
- The Boston Massacre by Theresa Shea.
- A Picture Book of Samuel Adams by David A. Adler.
- Why Don't You Get a Horse, Sam Adams? by Jean Fritz. We recommend everything by Jean Fritz.
- The Boston Massacre by Michael Burgan. History in graphic novel format.
- The Matchlock Gun by Walter D. Edmonds. Father goes off to war during the French and Indian War, leaving his young son to protect the family with their huge old Spanish musket. Read-aloud for younger kids.
- The Boston Tea Party by Russell Freedman.
- Johnny Tremain by Esther Forbes. A young boy gets caught up in the events of Boston in 1773 and has to choose between the Patriots and the Tories.
- Struggle for a Continent: The French and Indian Wars by Betsy Maestro.
- A Short, Easy History of the French and Indian Wars by Henry W. Elson.
- The Boston Massacre: An Interactive History Adventure by Elizabeth Raum.
- Samuel Adams and the Boston Tea Party by Gary Jeffrey. A graphic novel history.
- Indian Captive by Lois Lensky. A young girl is captured by Indians during the French and Indian War, her family is butchered, but she is raised among them.
- George Washington's World by Genevieve Foster. Takes a cross section of world history during the lifetime of George Washington. Highly recommended.
- French and Indian War Series by Joseph A. Altsheler. First published in 1916, this series of historical fiction novels takes place in North America during the French and Indian War. Available on Kindle.
- Under the Liberty Tree: A Story of the Boston Massacre by James Otis.
- Calico Captive by Elizabeth George Speare. A girl and her family are captured in an Indian raid during the French and Indian War.
- Countdown to Independence by Natalie S. Bober. Explains the events and arguments that led to the American War for Independence.
- The War That Made America: A Short History of the French and Indian War by Fred Anderson. Well written.
- Samuel Adams: Father of the American Revolution by Mark Puls.

HISTORY

BOSTON TEA PARTY – JAPAN – MORE REACTIONS – FOLK MUSIC

GEOGRAPHY	Search for: Japan, origami, Japanese folk tales ☺ <u>All About Japan: Songs, Stories, Crafts and More</u> by Willamarie Moore. ☺ <u>The Way We Do It In Japan</u> by Geneva Cobb Ilijima. ☺ <u>I Live In Tokyo</u> by Mari Takabayashi. ☺ <u>Japanese Celebrations: Cherry Blossoms, Lanterns, and Stars</u> by Betty Reynolds. ☺ ☺ <u>Japanese Children's Favorite Stories</u> by Florence Sakade. ☺ ☺ <u>A Treasury of Japanese Folktales</u> by Yuri Yasuda. ☺ ☺ <u>Japan: the Culture</u> by Bobbie Kalman. Look for other titles about Japan by this author. ☺ ☺ <u>Japan in Pictures</u> by Alison Behnke.
SCIENCE	Search for: chemistry, chemical reactions, chemistry experiments Books on individual chemistry topics do not exist for the most part. For high school we recommend you find a good general chemistry text and learn from it as you do the hands-on experiments from Layers of Learning. We frequently reference <u>Chemistry: A Self-Teaching Guide,</u> as well as <u>Khan Academy</u>. We also like <u>CK-12's</u> new science series which is free on Kindle and includes a high school chemistry text. For younger kids, just focus on experiments and what is happening in them along with some general chemistry books for younger kids or a science encyclopedia.
THE ARTS	Search for: folk music ☺ ☺ ☺ <u>Folk Songs of England, Ireland, and Wales</u> by William Cole. This is an actual songbook with sheet music for piano and guitar. ☺ ☺ ☺ <u>150 American Folk Songs to Sing, Read, and Play</u> by Peter Erdei and Katalin Komlos. A book of sheet music geared to teachers of elementary children. It includes games and activities that go along with the songs. ☺ ☺ ☺ <u>American Folk Songbook</u> by Suzy Bogguss. This is a CD, or you can get it via mp3 download on Amazon. Bogguss also wrote a companion book to this CD, by the same title, with stories about the songs and the artists, along with the sheet music to all of the songs on the album. ☺ ☺ ☺ <u>American Folk Songs For Children</u> by Mike and Peggy Seeger. If you buy only one album of folk songs, this should be it. There are 94 different folk songs and you can also buy the companion book <u>American Folk Songs for Children</u> by Ruth Seeger. ☺ <u>Passing the Music Down</u> by Sarah Sullivan. A picture book that tells the story of a fiddler who teaches a young boy his music so the boy can carry it on. ☺ <u>Wee Sing Fun 'n' Folk</u> by Pamela Conn Beall and Susan Hagan Nipp. This is a CD of folk songs with a book of lyrics so you can learn to sing along. ☺ ☺ <u>A Child's Celebration of Folk Music</u> by Music for Little People. An audio collection. ☺ <u>American Ballads and Folk Songs</u> by John A. Lomax and Alan Lomax. In the 1930's the authors went on a road trip and cataloged every American folk song they came across. This book describes the songs, and also includes lyrics and snippets of the melodies.

BOSTON TEA PARTY – JAPAN – MORE REACTIONS – FOLK MUSIC

HISTORY: BOSTON TEA PARTY

On the Web
This Schoolhouse Rock song "No More Kings" is a great introduction to the Boston Tea Party and the "taxation without representation" mantra of the colonists.
https://youtu.be/t-9pDZMRCpQ

Writer's Workshop
The events discussed in this section served as the catalyst for the colonists declaring independence and forming a free nation. The colonists recognized their rights and demanded them, whatever the cost. Do you think we've lost sight of the importance of our liberties? Write about liberty and what it's worth. Have we lost any of the rights they demanded?

On The Web
Learn more about the Boston Tea Party, see time lines, illustrations, and first hand accounts here:
http://www.boston-tea-party.org/index.html
Watch an interactive video here:
http://havefunwithhistory.com/activities/btp.html

On December 16, 1773 a bunch of citizens of Boston, fed up with the tax on tea, went into Boston Harbor, climbed aboard three vessels, and tossed all the tea overboard.

The problems between America and England began fifteen years earlier, in 1760, when King George III became king of England. The French and Indian War was nearing its end. The Seven Years' War was over. And the English needed money. Simultaneously, they realized that the American colonies were becoming quite populated and quite wealthy. The obvious answer was to tax.

The sugar tax went into effect. The Americans were not pleased. They protested, boycotted, and smuggled until the English caved. Now King George, who wanted to regain the power and prestige of the throne that his father and grandfather had lost, was not pleased. He was determined that the colonists would obey. For George, it had nothing to do with money and everything to do with fealty to the crown at any cost. For the colonists, it had nothing to do with money either. They believed that as Englishmen they had rights granted by the government, and as humans they had inherent rights given by God, both of which England was attempting to trample on. For Parliament, it really was about the money. They had bills to pay.

Over the next several years England and America had a tug of war. England taxed. America protested, sent nasty letters,

BOSTON TEA PARTY – JAPAN – MORE REACTIONS – FOLK MUSIC

threatened and assaulted the king's representatives, and boycotted taxed products. Back and forth, back and forth. Violence broke out occasionally, as in the Boston Massacre and the murder of an eleven year old boy by a British supporter. Violence occurred on both sides, but almost all of it was instigated by the Patriots. Boston was the worst, so Parliament sent troops to keep the peace in Boston.

Meanwhile, the men and women of the colonies were reading, writing letters, and having secret societies to discuss the problems, the solutions, and their beliefs about government. They were the most well-read and thoughtful people upon the subject ever in the history of the world. So when the time came to take a stand once again in Boston Harbor, they were ready. Tossing the tea in the harbor hurt the already financially struggling British East India Company immeasurably. It hurt the members of Parliament, who almost all had stake in the British East India Company as well. Plus it sent the firm message once again that this battle was not about the money, it was about whether the Americans were vassals and slaves of Britain or citizens with full rights of representation. The question would not be decided for some time after the Boston Tea Party, and the deciding would require the fortunes and blood of thousands of Patriots.

🙂 🙂 🙂 EXPLORATION: Timeline

At the end of this unit you will find printable timeline squares.
- 1754 French and Indian War begins
- 1759 British capture Quebec, turning point of the war
- 1763 Peace of Paris gives most North American land to the British
- 1764 Sugar Act, first tax intended to raise money for British debts
- 1764 Currency Act, preventing colonies from issuing their own currency
- 1764 First colonists protest in town meetings, organize protest societies, refuse to use imported British goods
- 1765 Quartering Act requires colonists to provide British soldiers with housing and food
- 1765 Stamp Act requires a tax stamp on all paper documents from marriage licenses to playing cards
- 1765 Sons of Liberty formed, colonies jointly issue official protest to Parliament against taxation without representation, use intimidation methods against British tax collectors
- 1766 Stamp Act is repealed; Declaratory Act, passed the same day as the Stamp Act repeal, stated that Parliament could

Explanation

The Boston Tea Party represents the people's refusal to be slaves to the government. It asserts that the people will be the masters, not the other way around. It is a testament to the power of a people to resist against great odds. Even Great Britain, the mighty country that had just defeated the nations of Europe, mastered the seas, and colonized around the globe, could not beat that handful of Patriots fighting for liberty.

Additional Layer

English people from this time period to read about:
- William Pitt
- King George III
- Lord North
- Edmund Burke
- Isaac Barre

Additional Layer

Americans from this time period to read about:
- Samuel Adams
- Paul Revere
- John Hancock
- Thomas Jefferson
- George Washington
- Abigail Adams
- John Adams
- Benjamin Franklin
- Mercy Otis Warren

Boston Tea Party – Japan – More Reactions – Folk Music

Additional Layer
Smuggling was big business at this time, in America and also in England. Nobody really likes to pay taxes, and shopkeepers do like to undercut the competition. Smuggling was so universally participated in by wealthy, middle class, and poor that customs payments were virtually unenforceable.

In fact, the Boston Tea Party was partly in response to the East India Company being given such a good deal by Parliament that they undercut the smugglers.

Famous Folks

Major General James Wolfe is famous for his victory over the French at Quebec in 1759 during the French and Indian War. He died in that battle and his death was dramatically portrayed by Benjamin West, American painter. Here is an explanation of both the event and the painting: https://youtu.be/VuQ5SzExJNc.

- make all laws for the colonies whatsoever
- 1767 Townshend Acts passed taxing lead, paint, glass, paper and tea
- 1767 Colonies practice non-importation against British goods, "Letters From a Farmer in Pennsylvania" published
- 1768 Samuel Adams wrote a letter on behalf of the Massachusetts Assembly protesting taxation and calling for unified resistance among the colonies; Parliament suspended the assembly in response
- 1769 Virginia stated that only the Virginia Assembly had the right to tax Virginia citizens
- 1770 Townshend Acts are withdrawn, except the tax on tea
- March 5, 1770 Boston Massacre
- 1772 Colonists attack a British Customs ship "Gaspee" in Rhode Island and the royal governor plans to send the men to trial in England, causing great uproar
- 1772 Samuel Adams forms first Committee of Correspondence in Massachusetts in order to communicate between colonial assemblies, other colonies follow suit
- 1773 Tea Act reduces tax on British tea merchants only, giving an unfair advantage, Colonists plan to boycott tea
- December 16, 1773 Boston Tea Party
- 1774 Intolerable Acts designed to punish Boston shut down the port of Boston, destroy the Massachusetts Charter, and change the court jurisdiction to England for all cases involving riots or revenue collection
- Sept 5, 1774 First Continental Congress of all the colonies meets in Philadelphia
- 1774 Massachusetts forms its own congressional body in defiance to the crown and prepares for war, creating the special militia unit known as the Minutemen
- 1775 Restraining Act: Parliament bans commerce between the Colonies and any other nation except England
- 1775 New England resists efforts of British troops to seize Colonial stores of ammunition, England decides armed force will be necessary
- 1775 Lexington and Concord: British move to take the ammunition at Concord, but are met by Minutemen, shots are fired and many die on both sides by the end of the day

☺ ☺ ☺ **EXPLORATION: French and Indian War**
The French and Indian War was part of a greater conflict between the British and the French. It was fought all over the world wherever the British and the French had colonies. In North America the two powers made alliances with local tribes. The Indians (allied with the French) would attack British frontier

settlements, scalping, killing, and carrying off captives. The British would then mount expeditions to attack Indian villages or French forts. Most of the fighting took place in the wilderness or along the frontier regions. The local colonists took part in the fighting in the form of militias risen for the purpose. The British also sent regular troops to fight. But the British were stretched thin, also fighting wars in Europe and India at the same time.

Control of the Ohio Valley was at the center of the fight. Whoever controlled the Ohio Valley controlled the rest of the land in the interior of the continent, and thereby, the rich fur trade. At first the French dealt blow after blow to the British. The colonists were afraid of the horrific Indian attacks. Then the young William Pitt was made Prime Minister, and he renewed British commitment to North America, sending in new troops and new commanders and giving the colonists free reign to form and manage their own militias. The war took a turn when Commander James Wolfe stormed a hill and took the city of Quebec. Wolfe died in the battle, but soon after, the French were completely driven from North America.

Both France and Britain were impoverished by the conflicts. In France it led to rising taxes and the eventual overthrow of the French monarchy. In Britain it also led to rising taxes and the loss of their most valuable region, the North American colonies.

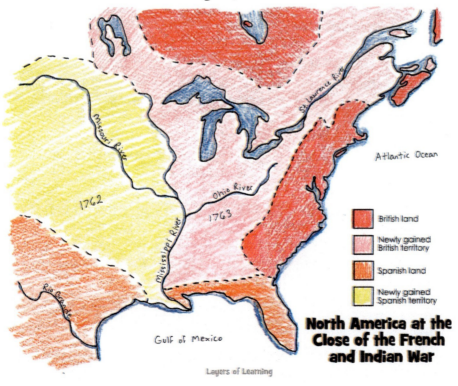

On the Web
Mr. Hughs, history teacher and occasional user of foul language, explains the French and Indian War:
https://youtu.be/VuQ5SzExJNc

On the Web
This 19 minute documentary about the results of the French and Indian War is worth a look.
https://youtu.be/Ktkw7iSITkc

Additional Layer
This is Faneuil Hall in Boston.

It was built by a wealthy merchant and slave trader, Peter Faneuil, for the city of Boston. The bottom floor was a marketplace and the upper floor was an assembly hall. It was the site of meetings of the Massachusetts Assembly and speeches by Samuel Adams, James Otis, and other rebels. Learn more about its history.

Boston Tea Party – Japan – More Reactions – Folk Music

Memorization Station

December 1773- The Boston Tea Party

Remember this date when free people stood up for their rights against tyranny and won.

Memorization Station

Read and memorize the poem *Revolutionary Tea*.

http://www.constitution.org/col/lyrics/revolutionary_tea.html

Make sure the kids understand the meaning of the poem. This poem is an allegory. "Old Mother" is Britain. The daughter is the colonies. The old lady's pockets represent the treasury of England. The old mother's servants are representatives of the crown.

Additional Layer

How important is it to be united in order to achieve the goals of your cause? Can a group that is splintered and arguing among itself win? How can a group that does not agree on 100% of their ideas unite? Relate this to your life, to a group you are involved with, or to a political movement you are aware of.

At the end of this unit you will find a map showing the British colonies and British gains during the French and Indian War. Color the map using the one above as a guide. Label the rivers and other waters. Write the date the new territories were acquired on the map.

☺ ☺ ☺ **EXPLORATION: United We Live**

During the war a printer in Philadelphia named Benjamin Franklin made this political cartoon for his paper.

It shows the various colonies split apart into sections of the snake. The message was clear – united the Colonies could prevail, but if they remained aloof and uncooperative with one another, they would die. This was the first time the concept of a united group of American Colonies had surfaced. The same cartoon and the same concept would be used later during the Revolutionary War to great effect.

Make a long snake, similar to this one, with construction paper. Cut it out and then paste the pieces down along the top edge only, labeling it the way Benjamin Franklin labeled his snake, with the various colonies. Flip up each piece and, on the back, write a little about the efforts each of these colonies made toward securing their rights from the British. Did they have protests? Meetings? Boycotts?

☺ ☺ **EXPLORATION: Taxation Without Representation**

The American colonists were citizens of Britain and they believed they had the same rights as all other British citizens, including the right to their own property. So when the British Parliament in London passed the tax bills known as the Sugar Act, the Stamp Act, and the Townshend Acts, each in turn, without the colonists having any say, they were upset. They didn't object to being taxed per se, they just thought they should only be taxed by a government where they had representatives who could vote on those taxes. They also thought that if they were taxed, the money should be used to run their colonies and not used for the people back in England or elsewhere in the British Empire.

Explain what representative government is with this object lesson.

1. Have the kids each decorate their own group of sugar cookies, five each. When they decorated the cookies they put work into them and now the cookies belong to them. *Who owns the cookies you decorated? Who should be able to take your cookies away from you?*
2. The teacher/parent now decrees that each child has to give up one cookie for the teacher's use. *How do you feel about having to give up one of your cookies? What if you just refuse to give up your cookie; what do you think might happen?*
3. Next, tell the kids that instead of giving up one cookie to the teacher, they will get to vote on whether to have a party later. If they decide to have a party they will need cookies and each child will have to give up one cookie. Take a vote on whether to have a party and voluntarily give up one cookie for the party. *Did it feel differently when you were being forced to give up a cookie as compared to when you voted to voluntarily give up a cookie? Which method preserves private property and the rights of individuals?*

☺ **EXPLORATION: Massachusetts Circular Letter**
In 1768, after the Townshend Acts, another attempt to tax the colonies, was made law. The Massachusetts House sent a petition to the king asking for help. The letter, written by Samuel Adams, was known as the *Massachusetts Circular Letter* because it was also sent to the other colonies. As a result of the letter the crown governor of Massachusetts dissolved the Massachusetts House, taking away the local colonial government of Massachusetts. Read the Massachusetts Circular Letter:
http://avalon.law.yale.edu/18th_century/mass_circ_let_1768.asp

In the letter Samuel Adams explained the problems the colonists were having and also proposed solutions. Write down each of the problems and solutions that are explained in the letter.

Teaching Tip
After completing the "Taxation Without Representation" cookie activity, some kids might challenge you when you give them orders. "I didn't vote for that!" Simply explain that representative government is only for people who are educated and have self control. Children are not in either of these categories and so they get told what to do. The same is actually true of adults of who do not have education or self control, they end up getting ruled over by others.

Famous Folks

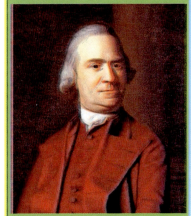

Samuel Adams was the central force behind the build up to the Revolution. His greatest accomplishment was probably the creation of the Committees of Correspondence. Learn more about it here:
https://youtu.be/wVnxtbQb5xc

BOSTON TEA PARTY – JAPAN – MORE REACTIONS – FOLK MUSIC

Additional Layer

British Law is based on common law, which means it grows out of decisions made one at a time by judges selected by the people. Essentially, the colonists were denied the protection of common law. Parliament and the king were instead trying to govern them as subjects under a dictator. The colonists were very aware of this.

Additional Layer

In 1772 Samuel Adams called for the formation of Committees of Correspondence in each of the 13 Colonies. The purpose was to facilitate communication between the Colonies about the problems with Britain. Adams knew that if the Colonies did not support one another and coordinate their efforts, then they would never be successful at securing their own freedom. The Committees of Correspondence also became illegal governments for each colony as their royal charters were revoked one by one. Eventually these committees would elect representatives to serve on the Continental Congresses, the first national government for the United States.

EXPLORATION: The Argument

For years before the Boston Tea Party, the British Parliament had been trying to tax the colonies in order to relieve the debt the British had acquired over the course of the Seven Years' War. Additionally, they were trying to aid the struggling British East India Company, of which the majority of Parliament were share holders. The British thought of the colonies as possessions, but the colonists, at least in America, thought of themselves as full British citizens with all the rights implied and stated in the Magna Carta and the much more recent British Bill of Rights (1689). The problem was that the British were not affording the colonists the right to govern themselves or the right to have full representation in Parliament. The colonists saw themselves as becoming mere slaves of England, so they fought back.

Early in the conflict a Philadelphia lawyer named John Dickinson explained clearly what the colonists were arguing for in a letter, first published in newspapers and then distributed in pamphlets throughout the colonies. Dickinson took a reasonable and moderate tone, not that of a violent radical. At this point few had any thought of breaking off from Britain entirely; they just wanted to be recognized as full Englishmen with all the rights of Englishmen.

Read John Dickinson's first letter, which he wrote anonymously as "Letters From a Farmer in Pennsylvania," which you can find here: http://www.earlyamerica.com/bookmarks/letters-pennsylvania-farmer/letters-from-a-pennsylvania-farmer-text/. As you read, pause and take notes about each of the arguments that Dickinson puts forth.

EXPLORATION: Rebellious Boston

The Townshend Acts required customs officials to inventory and tax goods coming into ports like Boston. But in Boston and other towns the locals were not willing to cooperate with the customs men on taxes they believed were wrong. So the customs officials asked for military support to enforce the law. Soldiers were sent to Boston. The Bostonians rioted. More soldiers were sent to Boston. Boston became a town under martial law.

By now the official government of Massachusetts had been suspended, but of course, that didn't stop the New Englanders. Boston convened its town hall and they called for the other town halls in Massachusetts to send representatives to meet at Faneuil Hall to discuss the problem of the Townshend Acts and the occupation of Boston. It was essentially an illegal government of Massachusetts. They wrote a letter condemning the occupation

Boston Tea Party – Japan – More Reactions – Folk Music

and calling it a violation of their English rights. Samuel Adams wrote many more letters protesting the occupation. Newspapers wrote daily commentaries of the incidents between the soldiers and civilians, many of them exaggerated. Two regiments were withdrawn, but two more remained. Tensions between the soldiers and citizens rose higher and higher.

At the end of this unit you will find a printable Faneuil Hall model. We recommend you copy it on to card stock. Color it. The hall was built of red brick with white trim. Cut it out around the perimeter of the piece. Turn it over and on the back write the names of people who were part of the resistance movement in Boston, things they said, and things they did. Then fold the craft along the solid lines. Glue together with the tabs.

😊 😊 😊 EXPLORATION: Boston Massacre

On March 5, 1770 a crowd gathered in front of the Customs House on King Street in Boston. A lone British sentry stood guarding the door. The crowd, angry over the presence of soldiers in their town and looking for a fight, taunted and threatened the young private. Seven more soldiers and an officer joined the guard. The crowd continued their abusive language and began to throw things at the soldiers including snowballs with oyster shells embedded in them. More and more people joined the crowd until there were more than three hundred Bostonians facing off against the seven British soldiers and their officer. Finally, one soldier was struck and knocked down by a stick wielded by a member of the crowd. The soldier roared back to his feet shouting for the men to fire. He then fired into the crowd, after which eleven more shots were fired, though the officer had never given the order. Three men lay dead and many others were wounded, some of them later dying of their wounds.

This was an engraving done by Paul Revere and used for propaganda to fuel responses and outrage against the British.

The soldiers and their officer were put on trial. John Adams represented them after finding that no other Bostonian would do it and believing firmly in the rule of law. The officer and six of the men

> **Writer's Workshop**
> Write your own newspaper article describing the events of the Boston Tea Party. You could include a political cartoon as well.

> **Additional Layer**
> The British constitution consists of many different documents written over time. It is, in fact, the whole body of British law. It includes the Magna Carta of 1215, the 1689 Bill of Rights, and many other documents, judicial decisions, decrees of Parliament, and statutes. The American colonists were basing their concept of their rights on the whole of British law, especially on the 1689 Bill of Rights, which you can read here: http://avalon.law.yale.edu/17th_century/england.asp.

> **Additional Layer**
> Between 1765 and 1769 William Blackstone, English lawyer, wrote a treatise on English law called *Commentaries on the Laws of England*. It was hugely influential in America. Nearly all of the founders read it and they modeled their ideas of law and government after the principles in it.

Boston Tea Party – Japan – More Reactions – Folk Music

Additional Layer
This is a clip showing John Adams giving the closing testimony in defense of the British soldiers accused of murder at the Boston Massacre: https://youtu.be/SiCEyuIuwAU

Famous Folks
Crispus Attucks was the first person killed at the Boston Massacre and is often considered the first fatality of the Revolution even though the war didn't start for two years after this.

On the Web
This is the full "Liberty's Kids" episode of the Boston Tea Party: https://youtu.be/GJ-FWHN3ljI.

This is the first in this series. It goes on through the whole Revolutionary period.

were acquitted and the remaining two men were given a reduced sentence of manslaughter with a punishment of branding on the thumbs.

The events of the Boston Massacre were used to fuel more fire for the Patriot cause. They also forced the removal of the troops from Boston.

Read these accounts of the Boston Massacre:
- Theodore Bliss, a Boston citizen: http://www.bostonmassacre.net/trial/d-bliss.htm
- Captain Thomas Preston, British officer: http://www.bostonmassacre.net/trial/acct-preston1.htm
- A modern reenactment of the event: https://youtu.be/-K2UgQFRr38

Finally, make puppets depicting the British soldiers and men of Boston and make your own reenactment of events. We suggest figures drawn and attached to wooden craft sticks as puppets.

☺ ☺ ☺ EXPLORATION: Boston Tea Party
In December of 1773 colonists disguised as Indians boarded a British East India ship and threw all the tea overboard in protest over British tyranny.

Read this account from the Massachusetts Gazette published in 1773, immediately after the Tea Party. Then re-enact the Tea Party for yourself with Indian costumes and all. You can use this script written for children if you like: http://www.kidsinco.com/2012-/01/the-boston-tea-party/

Boston Tea Party – Japan – More Reactions – Folk Music

WHILE a public meeting was being held, to protest against the tea ships, a number of brave and resolute men, dressed in the Indian manner, approached near the door of the assembly. They gave a war whoop, which rang through the house and was answered by some in the galleries; but silence was commanded and a peaceable behaviour until the end of the meeting.

The Indians, as they were then called, repaired to the wharf, where the ships lay that had the tea on board. They were followed by hundreds of people to see the event of the transactions of those who made so grotesque an appearance.

The Indians immediately repaired on board Captain Hall's ship, where they hoisted out the chests of tea. When on deck they stove them and emptied the tea overboard.

Having cleared this ship they proceeded to Captain Bruce's, and then to Captain Coffin's brig. They applied themselves so dexterously to the destruction of this commodity, that in the space of three hours they broke up three hundred and forty-two chests, which was the whole number of these vessels, and poured their contents into the harbor.

When the tide rose it floated the broken chests and the tea. The surface of the water was filled therewith a considerable way from the south part of the town to Dorchester Neck and lodged on the shores.

The greatest care was taken to prevent the tea from being purloined by the populace. One or two who were detected trying to pocket a small quantity were stripped of their plunder and very roughly handled.

It is worthy of remark that although a considerable quantity of

Additional Layer

Just before the Boston Tea Party the British Parliament had enacted new legislation that would've undercut the price of tea smuggled into the Colonies. The more radical colonists, especially those in Boston, were still forcing a boycott of tea because of the Townshend Acts, which had been repealed except the tax on tea. They couldn't allow the tea to land or their boycott would fail. Read more about it here:

http://www.boston-tea-party.org/tea-act.html.

Fabulous Fact

Other cities besides Boston held tea parties as well, including New York, Greenwich, New Jersey, and Annapolis, Maryland.

Fabulous Facts

The destruction of the tea at Boston cost the already suffering British East India Company about $1.7 million in today's dollars. It also made drinking tea into an unpatriotic activity and virtually destroyed the tea market in the U.S. up to the present day. Americans are still coffee drinkers.

BOSTON TEA PARTY – JAPAN – MORE REACTIONS – FOLK MUSIC

Additional Layer

Many Americans of the day, including George Washington, disagreed with the destruction of the tea at Boston, but they united against Britain's reaction to the Tea Party. Britain passed several laws such as closing the port of Boston, annulling colonial self government in Massachusetts, and expanding the quartering of soldiers. These new laws together were dubbed "Intolerable Acts" by the colonists.

Learn more about the Intolerable Acts and how they helped to unite America.

Consider how the reaction to behavior that someone disagrees with can be a bigger problem than the behavior in the first place.

Additional Layer

This poem was written following the Boston Tea Party in December of 1773.
http://www.loc.gov/pictures/resource/cph.3a50224/
What does it mean to be Free-born? Free to do what? Why were the people of Boston willing to risk their lives and possessions for freedom? What is a tyrant?

other goods were still remaining on board the vessel, no injury was sustained.

Such attention to private property was observed that when a small padlock belonging to the captain of one of the ships was broken, another was procured and sent to him.

The town was very quiet during the whole evening and the night following. Those who were from the country went home with a merry heart, and the next day joy appeared in almost every countenance, some on account of the destruction of the tea, others on account of the quietness with which it was done. One of the Monday's papers says that the masters and owners are well pleased that their ships are thus cleared, without their being responsible.

☺ ☺ ☺ **EXPLORATION: Boston Tea Party Poster**
Make a three sided display all about the Boston Tea Party. Include quotes, poems, images, and information about the events. Use three pieces of poster board. On one panel tell about the events of the Boston Tea Party, on another tell about the Sons of Liberty, on a third tell how the Boston Tea Party led the colonies toward war. Or do another three part display about this time period.

☺ ☺ **EXPLORATION: Tea Party Diorama**
Make a diorama of the Boston Tea Party in a shoe box. At the end of this unit you will find some printable figures and background pieces to include in your diorama. Paint the background inside

Boston Tea Party – Japan – More Reactions – Folk Music

the box to show Long Wharf and the Boston skyline. Add construction paper waves to represent the bay.

☺ ☺ ☺ **EXPLORATION: Minutemen**

Every man between the ages of 16 and 60 was required to train and be a member of the militia in the Colonies. Out of these ranks, certain younger men were selected to be a rapid response team. They were known as minutemen because they were ready in a "minute" to respond if they were needed. They were better trained than the regular militia, and throughout the Revolutionary War they were an important asset to the Patriot effort.

Copy the first stanza of Ralph Waldo Emerson's Concord Hymn onto a piece of paper. Illustrate it with a scene of the minutemen standing at Concord when the British came to take the ammunition depot.

> *By the rude bridge that arched the flood,*
> *Their flag to April's breeze unfurled,*
> *Here once the embattled farmers stood,*
> *And fired the shot heard round the world.*

Additional Layer

The Tea Party has been invoked many times by different people over the more than two centuries since it happened. Gandhi once pulled a handful of un-taxed salt from his pocket in the presence of a British official saying it was in memory of the Boston Tea Party.

Additional Layer

This is the Minuteman missile.

It was designed to carry up to three nuclear warheads and to be deployed at a moment's notice. This missile was and is instrumental in keeping the bad guys at bay. As long as we have it, are willing to use it, and can retaliate against aggression with overwhelming force, no one dares oppose the United States. This missile has the potential to keep the peace for the whole world merely by existing.

BOSTON TEA PARTY – JAPAN – MORE REACTIONS – FOLK MUSIC

GEOGRAPHY: JAPAN

Fabulous Fact

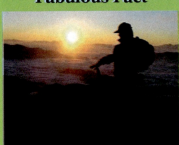

The Japanese characters that make up the name of Japan mean "sun origin." Japan is known as the land of the rising sun. Japan is situated to the east of China and is therefore the land where the sun rises.

On the Web

Watch this 30 minute documentary about Japan:
https://youtu.be/-pgCPJSiKo0

Additional Layer

Japan is a constitutional monarchy, but the role of the emperor is ceremonial only. Learn more about the Japanese government and influences from China, Germany, and the United States.

Vocabulary

archipelago
island
temperate
volcanic

Japan is a series of 6,852 islands in the North Pacific to the east of China. The islands are volcanic in origin and Japan experiences frequent earthquakes, eruptions, and tsunamis. Japan has the tenth largest population in the world, with over 127 million people and one of the world's highest population densities. Tokyo is the largest urban center of any place on the planet.

This is Tokyo, the capital of Japan. 38.7 million people live in the greater Tokyo area. Photo by Zaida Montañana, CC license, Wikimedia.

Japan is a highly developed country with the 3rd largest GDP in the world, the world's longest life expectancy, low homicide rates, and very low infant mortality. Japan is a member of the G8, a group of eight of the world's largest governments in terms of economy, and part of the UN, acting as a temporary member of the security council.

In 1947, following the Japanese defeat in World War II, the formerly militaristic government was defined according to U.S. dictates. The country adopted a written constitution, a bicameral parliament, and a prime minister. Japan was also legally denied the privilege of ever declaring war, though they do maintain a state-of-the art modern military for defense and peacekeeping purposes. There is still an emperor and Japan is officially a constitutional monarchy, but the emperor is, by law, merely a figurehead and symbol of national unity.

BOSTON TEA PARTY – JAPAN – MORE REACTIONS – FOLK MUSIC

☺ ☺ ☺ **EXPLORATION: Japan Map**
Color and label the map of Japan you will find at the end of this unit. Use a student atlas to find these places:

- Sea of Japan
- East China Sea
- Pacific Ocean
- Hokkaido Island
- Honshu Island
- Shikoku Island
- Kyushu Island
- Tokyo
- Osaka
- Kyoto
- Kobe
- Hiroshima
- Kumamoto
- Sapporo
- Sendai
- Mount Fuji

☺ ☺ ☺ **EXPLORATION: Hot Tubbin' With The Macaque**
Japan is mostly mountains, about 70 percent in fact, most of which are volcanoes. There is a monkey called the Japanese Macaque Monkey that lives in the colder, snowy parts of these volcanic mountains. They have found a way to keep warm in their snowy climate by soaking in the warm volcanic springs.

Photo by Yosemite, CC license, Wikimedia

Read about Macaque monkeys online, then choose one of these projects to accompany your reading:
- Japan sits right along the ring of fire, an area of volcanic and earthquake activity due to movement of the earth's plates. Read about and then map the ring of fire.
- Create a volcano. Salt dough or chicken wire and paper mache

Additional Layer

Formed of volcanoes, Japan is extremely mountainous and forested. Only about 30% of the land is habitable, so the people live very close together in the coastal areas.

This 6 minute video describes the geography of Japan: https://youtu.be/Ob7UhHBI7Oc.

Famous Folks

This is Emperor Akihito of Japan.

He became emperor in 1989, the 125th in his line. This is the oldest imperial family in the world. By law the Japanese Emperor can have no real political power or even influence on the government. His role is symbolic only. So the Emperor of Japan spends his time publishing scientific papers on ichthyology, fish.

BOSTON TEA PARTY – JAPAN – MORE REACTIONS – FOLK MUSIC

Additional Layer

You may want to learn more about one of these other animals that lives in Japan:

    Ussuri brown bear

    Amami rabbit

    Bonin flying fox

    Sika deer

    Japanese wild boar

    Japanese raccoon dog

Additional Layer

Japan is home to tens of thousands of Shinto shrines. Inside the shrines are housed sacred objects. Or sometimes the shrine stands on sacred ground, like a mountain, which is worshiped instead of an object in the shrine.

A Japanese shrine. Photo by Njo, Wikimedia, CC license

Learn more about the Shinto beliefs of Japan.

On the Web

This site has a printable Japanese shrine craft: http://www.busybeekidscrafts.com/Floating-Torii.html.

form a great base. Baking soda and vinegar combined with red food coloring create the terrific lava explosion.
- Write a creative story about what it would be like to swim with Japanese Macaque monkeys in the hot springs.
- Make a poster about another interesting animal that lives in Japan. Go to the library to do research. Do an oral presentation with a visual aid you create.
- Make a mini-book about other ways animals keep warm in cold climates. A new animal could be drawn on each page with an explanation of how they keep warm (polar bears, whales, and penguins are obvious choices, but there are many animals you could use.)

🙂 🙂 🙂 **EXPEDITION: Japanese Gardens**

Japanese gardens are highly stylized miniaturized landscapes. The art of creating perfect gardens for relaxation is an old one in Japan, dating back to the 700's AD.

The gardens always include water or a representation of water, such as white sand in a dry rock garden. The water and the stone in a garden are the ying and the yang, opposites that create a unified whole in Buddhist tradition. Brightly colored orange, yellow and red carp are often placed in Japanese gardens. Ponds are irregularly shaped and, where possible, there are cascades of running water. An island in the center of a pond represents Mount Horai, the home of the Eight Immortals. A vertical rock in the garden also could represent Mount Horai. The placement of rocks, sand, water, and plants is carefully chosen, but should seem to be random and natural. Often there are bridges,

Boston Tea Party – Japan – More Reactions – Folk Music

pavilions, or small buildings in gardens, but these too should blend into the landscape.

There are over 300 public Japanese gardens in the United States. Look for one near you and visit it. You can also make your own miniature Japanese garden in a shoebox. Use colored paper, paints, pebbles, and bits of greenery to decorate your garden.

☺ ☺ ☺ EXPLORATION: Origami

Origami is Japanese paper folding, and it's really fun. The word origami comes from two Japanese words - *oru*, meaning to fold, and *kami*, meaning paper. No one knows exactly when it started, but we do know it's been around for a long, long time. The Chinese invented paper, and then Buddhist monks brought it with them to Japan in the 5th century AD. The Japanese elevated simple paper folding into a beautiful art form. There are tons of tutorials online. You can also find origami books at your library.

Here is a picture tutorial for how to fold a paper crane. It is probably the best known origami figure. They say that if you fold 1,000 of them you will be granted a wish.

On the Web
This is a video tour of the Portand Japanese gardens:
https://youtu.be/LEKgHLxcFxM

Additional Layer
The population of Japan is homogeneous, with the same culture, race, history, and language.

How is a homogeneous population different from a multicultural one like the U.S.? Make a Venn diagram to compare the social benefits and problems under each.

Boston Tea Party – Japan – More Reactions – Folk Music

Fabulous Facts

Omamori are amulets sold at Japanese shrines. They are said to bestow good luck or protection. Japanese people get a new one each year and return the old one to be respectfully disposed of by the temple or shrine priests.

Famous Folks

After WWII the Japanese economy was devastated. People were hungry and the only thing to feed them was American bread, an unfamiliar food to the Japanese. So an entrepreneur named Momofuku Ando decided to come up with a way to mass produce inexpensive and easy to prepare noodles. He named his invention Top Ramen. Later he came up with Cup O' Noodles, an innovative package design in a Styrofoam cup to which one just adds hot water. His noodles have fed millions of poverty stricken people and disaster victims as well as poor college students.

😊 🟢 EXPLORATION: Koi Windsock

Koi windsocks are flown in Japan on May 5, which is Children's Day. Children's Day celebrates children, much like Mother's Day celebrates mothers or Father's Day celebrates fathers. You can make your own koi windsock to fly using markers, scissors, posterboard, a stapler, a hole punch, and some string.

Decorate your posterboard like a colorful koi fish that is rolled out flat. We trimmed a scalloped edge on the tail end and made patterned scales using markers. Then roll it up and staple each side, forming a cylinder. Finally, punch 4 holes around the top edge and attach strings to hang your windsock.

😊 🟢 EXPLORATION: Japanese Fans

The folding fan was invented in Japan more than a thousand years ago. The more sticks you had in your fan, the higher your rank. These fans were made of wood with fabric coverings and painted with nature scenes in soft watercolors. To make a fan you will need a piece of paper, two craft sticks, and paints or markers.

1. Fold a piece of white typing paper in half the long way, hot dog style. Then unfold it and cut along the fold line.
2. Tape the papers together end to end to make one long thin piece of paper.
3. Color or paint a nature scene on the paper. Let it dry.
4. Fold the paper accordion style, starting at one short end.
5. Tape one craft stick to either end of the paper, letting the sticks hang down about an inch and a half below the edge of the paper. Gather the paper at the other end, opposite the protruding craft sticks, and tape the paper firmly.

Boston Tea Party – Japan – More Reactions – Folk Music

6. Fold the paper up and grasp the sticks, pulling them around in a circle to make a fan shape.

😊 😊 EXPLORATION: Kokeshi

Kokeshi are Japanese dolls that were probably first made to sell to tourists who were visiting the hot springs in northern Japan in the 1600's. The dolls are simply shaped cylinders with no arms or legs, a few lines to define the face, and a floral painted dress.

At the end of this unit you will find some printable Kokeshi dolls. Four of them have faces and some simple designs on their clothes. Two of them have been left blank so you can draw in your own

Fabulous Fact

Noh is a traditional Japanese form of theater. Learn more about it.

Fabulous Fact

Japanese legend says that a Koi that swims upstream becomes a dragon. Koi windsocks appear to be swimming upstream in the wind.

Famous Folks

Ichiro Suzuki plays Major League Baseball. He started his career in Japan and came to America to play for the Mariners in 2001.

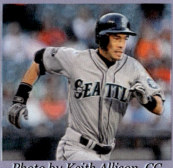

Photo by Keith Allison, CC license, Wikimedia

Boston Tea Party – Japan – More Reactions – Folk Music

On the Web

The most popular Japanese art form has to be Manga, Japanese animation that has swept the world. Your kids can get some free tutorials on how to draw their favorite style at www.howtodrawmanga.com.

Fabulous Fact

Japanese samurai used fans in war. The most common use was as a way to signal their troops during a battle. But fans were also used as weapons. They had steel ribs and lacquered fabric. Often the ribs were sharpened into points.

You can see the war fan in action here: https://youtu.be/xrzjh6bh9fI

Famous Folks

The legend of the 47 Ronin is a true historical event of 47 leaderless samurai (ronin) who revenged the forced suicide of their master. The story is part of the cultural heritage of Japan and illustrates a part of Japanese character: self-sacrifice, honor, loyalty, and persistence.

Watch the 2013 film *47 Ronin* with your older teens. It is violent, so be warned.

---

faces and designs. Color them, cut out the rectangles and glue them into a cylinder so they can stand.

☺ ☺ ☺ **EXPLORATION: Cherry Blossom Festival**

Every year in the spring when the cherry trees bloom, the Japanese have festivals. There are picnics and parties under the blooming trees. Lanterns are hung from the branches. In the past, members of the emperor's court would write poems about the blossoms.

Make a cherry blossom painting. You need a large white piece of paper, dark brown paint, and pink tissue paper. Paint a tree trunk and thin dark branches. Let the paint dry, then dab dots of glue over the branches and stick small crumpled squares of pink tissue paper to each of the glue dots.

Now write a Haiku to the cherry blossoms. Haiku is a Japanese form of poetry. It has three lines. The first line has five syllables, the second has seven, and the final line has five.

> Creamy pink blossoms
> Standing stark against the sky
> Wait for buzzing bees.

Write your Haiku, in very nice handwriting, right on your cherry blossom painting.

Boston Tea Party – Japan – More Reactions – Folk Music

☺ ☺ ☺ EXPLORATION: Sumi-e
Sumi-e is an old art form in Japan where the artist uses a bamboo brush and black ink on rice paper to make simple but profound images of a natural scene or objects.

Look up some examples of Sumi-e online and consider getting an inexpensive kit from Amazon to try it out. We like the Sumi-e Kit by Shingo Syoko which sells for less than $8.

☺ ☺ ☺ EXPLORATION: Kimono Report
At the end of this unit you will find a printable kimono report form. Print it onto heavy paper. Fold along the solid vertical lines to fold the two sides of the kimono in. Decorate the outside. Inside the kimono flaps write a report or list facts about Japan.

☺ ☺ ☺ EXPLORATION: Okonomiyaki
Okonomiyaki means "whatever you like, grilled" in Japanese. Years ago some foreign exchange students from Japan taught our family to make this version. There are no exact recipes, because the ingredients literally include whatever you like.

Additional Layer

Japan is a huge innovator and exporter of high tech goods. They lead the world in robotics and are major contributors in automobiles, biotechnology, optics, and superconductors.

Japan has the third largest economy in the world and has a standard of living comparable with the United States.

Japan achieved this from a position of economic devastation and almost total annihilation of infrastructure and political structure following WWII. The 1960's to the 1980's in Japan are called the "economic miracle." Find out how they did it and then apply the principles to a poor nation in the world today. How might a poor nation be turned into a wealthy one?

Additional Layer

Listen to this traditional Japanese music with a very modern twist: https://youtu.be/eNoDyfvABHc.

It sort of says everything about Japan. . . 3,000 years of culture married with the most modern of people.

Boston Tea Party – Japan – More Reactions – Folk Music

Fabulous Fact

The kimono is the traditional dress for both men and women in Japan. Today only older women, sumo wrestlers, who must wear traditional dress in public, and people who are involved in special occasions, like festivals or weddings, wear kimonos. Everyone else wears western style clothing.

On the Web

Watch this 26 minute show about Japanese cuisine. Yum!

https://youtu.be/2xzTbDGKpAA

You can find many more recipes to cook and try for yourself here: http://www.japanesecooking101.com/.

Begin by combining a variety of vegetables, chopped into tiny pieces, into a large mixing bowl. You can even use a food processor to chop the veggies if you want. We use:

1/4 of a cabbage
2 carrots
1 onion
6-8 florets of broccoli
Shrimp or chicken, diced up small (optional, we normally use veggies only)

Next, you'll make the batter by combining these ingredients into a bowl:
2 cups flour
6 eggs
1 tsp. salt
Water – just add it in bit by bit until the batter becomes the consistency of thick pancake batter

Now combine the vegetables with the batter, making sure the vegetables are well coated. Stir everything well. If you have too much batter, just chop up a few more veggies. If your vegetables aren't well coated, whip up a little extra batter.

Once your batter is ready, splash about ¼ cup of oil in a frying pan and spoon your batter into pancake size circles. Put a lid on top. Let them cook until browned well, then flip them over, put the lid back on and let the other side brown. You want to make sure to cover them with a lid so the vegetables and insides get well cooked and warmed. When both sides are browned, remove them from the heat and serve them right away.

BOSTON TEA PARTY – JAPAN – MORE REACTIONS – FOLK MUSIC

Serve them with a fifty-fifty combination of mayonnaise and a good teriyaki sauce. Our favorite sauce is Yoshida's Sauce.

☺ ☻ ☺ **EXPLORATION: Japan Book Project**
Read *Sadako and the Thousand Paper Cranes* by Eleanor Coerr, *The Big Wave* by Pearl S. Buck, or *Hachiko: The True Story of a Loyal Dog* by Pamela Turner. Make a book project based on the book you read.

☺ ☻ ☺ **EXPLORATION: Cultural Rules**
Every country has their own set of cultural rules and norms. Here are some that apply in Japan:
- When you go inside, you always remove your shoes. You should be wearing clean socks. Your host will also provide house slippers for you to wear while you stay. When your shoes are removed, you should place them neatly with the toes pointing toward the door.
- When you go into the bathroom there will be a special pair of toilet slippers to wear that should only be worn in the restroom.
- Japanese baths are for both cleanliness and relaxation. The tubs are in a separate room than the toilet. First, you shower to get clean, then get into the hot bath. Once you've soaked and relaxed, you get out and soap up, then rinse off. Finally, you end with a final soak in the tub.
- Everyone generally begins eating a meal at the same time, so if some has not yet received their food, it is polite to wait. Before you begin eating, say "itadakimasu" (I gratefully receive). Small dishes are picked up and held up near your mouth, but larger dishes should remain on the table. Chopsticks are the primary utensils used. It is polite to finish every single bit of food on your plate. When the meal is finished, all the dishes should be returned to their original placement, with lids on pots and chopsticks on their holders.
- Sitting on the floor is common in Japan, even while eating meals. They use low tables and everyone sits directly on the floor. Men sit cross legged while women sit with their legs to one side. It is acceptable for both men and women to kneel as well.
- Giving gifts is an important part of Japanese culture. Gifts are given frequently to guests, and also family, friends, and coworkers. They are always wrapped and both the giver and receiver must make the exchange with both hands.

Have a special dinner and practice all these rules of etiquette while you dine.

Teaching Tip
Let kids choose their own book project. For a list of ideas, go visit *Karen's Big List of Book Projects* on the Bookworms Page at Layers of Learning.

http://www.layers-of-learning.com/karens-big-list-of-book-projects/

Additional Layer
On the first day of the New Year Japanese people visit a shrine, throw a coin in, and make a wish for the New Year. This holiday is called Hatsumode.

This video shows how to participate in Hatsumode:
https://youtu.be/93NhRo_fAJM.

And this video shows Japanese people celebrating and praying on the New Year:
https://youtu.be/CjS_iam9peI.

Fabulous Fact
Japan has both western toilets (the kind you're probably used to) and squat toilets (which is basically a hole in the ground). You squat low over the hole to use the restroom. These are considered more sanitary because the toilet never touches your skin.

BOSTON TEA PARTY – JAPAN – MORE REACTIONS – FOLK MUSIC

SCIENCE: MORE REACTIONS

On the Web

Here is an excellent video lecture from Mr. Anderson on reversible reactions to watch before you do the experiments:

https://youtu.be/b6WmwtVNDf4

Famous Folks

Berthollet discovered chlorine could be used as a bleach. You have him to thank for your bright whites in the laundry. He was also one of the scientists who traveled to Egypt with Napoleon.

Additional Layer

Design your own experiment based on Berthollet's observation of the super-saturated lake.

Teaching Tip

Food works every time. Make some non-reversible cake or brownies as a yummy introduction to this unit.

Most reactions once done are done. You can't take apart a cake you baked and get back out the flour, the eggs, the oil, the sugar, the baking powder, and so on. But some reactions are reversible. You can change the reaction back the other direction and get what you started with. This was first discovered in 1803 by Claude Louis Berthollet, a French chemist. He noticed that solid salts formed at the edge of salt lakes and saw that the salts that were dissolved could be made solid again. The reaction he saw was:

$$2NaCl + CaCO_3 \rightarrow Na_2CO_3 + CaCl_2.$$
sodium chloride + calcium carbonate → sodium carbonate + calcium chloride
Table salt + limestone chalk → washing soda + road salt

Reactions happen at different speeds depending on conditions. The speed a reaction occurs at is called the rate. A rate of reaction can be sped up or slowed down by temperature, pressure, or mechanical means. Sometimes chemical means can be used to speed up or start a reaction. A chemical that gets a reaction going or speeds it up is called a catalyst. A catalyst that works inside a living organism is called an enzyme.

🙂 🟢 **EXPLORATION: Reversible Processes**
This set of demonstrations will help younger kids to understand the concept of reversing processes, but these are not reactions, for

Boston Tea Party – Japan – More Reactions – Folk Music

the most part, since the chemical makeup of the substances never changes. This activity will also help kids practice problem solving and deduction skills.

Tell the kids you're going to give them some chemicals that they have to change back to their original form. Ask them to figure out how to reverse the process. One of the processes cannot be reversed, which is it?

1. Melt an ice cube and get back ice (freezing)
2. Dissolve salt in water and get the salt back out (evaporation)
3. Flour mixed into water, get the flour back out (filter)
4. Bake a cake and get back your original ingredients.

☺ ☺ ☺ **EXPERIMENT: Magic Blue Bottle**

This can be used as a demonstration for younger kids or for older kids to do on their own with supervision.

CAUTION: Wear gloves and eye protection when handling these chemicals. Sodium Hydroxide is extremely dangerous. Methylene blue will stain clothes, counters, dish towels, skin, etc. To dispose of these chemicals after the experiment, flood with vinegar to neutralize the sodium hydroxide, then wash down the sink with plenty of water.

You need:
- Methylene Blue (Home Science Tools)
- Sodium Hydroxide (Home Science Tools or in some drain cleaners, read ingredients list)
- Distilled water (automotive)
- Crystalline Fructose (health food store/section) or Dextrose (Home Science Tools)
- Clean clear glass or plastic jar with a lid or flask with a stopper

Procedure:
1. Make a solution of the sodium hydroxide by adding 3 tsp. of sodium hydroxide to 100 ml (½ c.) of distilled water; stir to dissolve as much as possible. **Very dangerous, beware of splashes! This step is exothermic; it will produce heat!**
2. Add the sodium hydroxide solution to a clear glass or plastic jar or flask that has a lid or stopper.
3. Carefully add one drop of methylene blue to the flask.
4. Measure 1 g (1 tsp.) of fructose and add it to the flask, gently swirling to dissolve.

Additional Layer

Find out what kinds of everyday substances contain or are made of calcium carbonate.

Definition

A reversible reaction is a chemical reaction where the reactants and products reach equilibrium. It can be expressed like this

$$A + B \leftrightarrow C + D$$

Two reactants, A and B, combine in some way to make two new products, C and D. But C and D also react to make A and B.

On the Web

You can always watch most of these experiments on the web. . . but there's nothing like actually making it yourself.

Here's the blue bottle experiment: https://youtu.be/a_4LUaaL6FU

BOSTON TEA PARTY – JAPAN – MORE REACTIONS – FOLK MUSIC

Additional Layer
Try adding table salt and calcium carbonate to water in large amounts until it comes back out of solution. Use a little water and lots of salt and calcium carbonate, then let your water evaporate. Notice that in the chemical equation in the introduction to this unit the salt to calcium carbonate ratio is 2 to 1. Use the scientific method when designing your experiment and take good notes and record your observations.

Additional Layer
In the green to blue reaction, it looks like the reaction stops, but actually it's going both backward and forward at the same time all the time, it's just that the equilibrium settles in either the blue camp or the green camp depending on the proportions of the reactants. Learn more about equilibrium.

Additional Layer
Le Chatelier's Principle explains why some reactions can be reversed. You can learn about it with Khan Academy:
https://youtu.be/4-fEvpVNTlE

5. Place the lid on the jar and shake violently. This adds oxygen from the air to the solution and should make the solution turn blue.
6. Let the solution stand for a few minutes and it will turn back to clear.

The methylene blue is an indicator that turns clear if it has extra electrons and blue if it has fewer electrons (a redox indicator). When shaking the solution, oxygen from the air is dissolved in the water and the oxygen snaps up the electrons from the fructose when it is in a strongly alkaline solution. As the solution sits, the oxygen is overcome once more and electrons return to the water. This is a reversible reaction. We'll cover oxidation and reduction more in Unit 3-19.

Here's the equation:

$$\text{Fructose} + \text{Oxygen} \rightleftharpoons \text{Carbon Dioxide} + \text{water}$$
$$C_6H_{12}O_6 + O_2 \rightleftharpoons CO_2 + H_2O$$

The sodium hydroxide is a catalyst that helps to rip electrons off the fructose. The methylene blue is also combining with the fructose electrons, but there's so little of it that we're only interested in it for the color it turns, letting us know the reaction is taking place. If you use too much methylene blue your experiment won't work.

☻ **EXPERIMENT: Green To Blue and Back Again**
This reaction will show how sometimes you can reverse the process and get back what you started. You will be able to switch back and forth between a green and blue solution as you add chemicals.

CAUTION: Copper sulfate, ammonia and hydrochloric acid are all corrosive and dangerous chemicals. You must wear safety goggles and gloves when performing this experiment. The experiment must be in a well

Boston Tea Party – Japan – More Reactions – Folk Music

ventilated area and adult supervision is required. This experiment is for older students only.

You need:
- Copper sulfate (Home Science Tools)
- Ammonia (cleaning aisle)
- Hydrochloric acid (Home Science tools)

Procedure:
1. Make a copper sulfate solution by first crushing ¼ tsp. of the copper sulfate crystals into powder and adding the powder to ¼ cup of distilled water (you can buy distilled water in automotive). Stir.
2. Add 10 ml copper sulfate solution to a test tube. It should be light blue.
3. Add 25 ml of hydrochloric acid to the test tube and gently swirl to stir. The solution will turn green. **When the acid is added fumes will be produced. Hold the test tube near an open window or ventilation hood and away from people.**
4. Add 25 ml of ammonia to the test tube, do not stir. Wait for the solution to turn dark blue. Add a little more ammonia if the solution does not turn.
5. After the solution has turned dark blue add a little hydrochloric acid to turn it green again.

Here is what happens:
copper sulfate (aq) + Chlorine → Copper Chloride + water
$$[Cu(H_2O)_6]^{2+} + Cl^- \rightarrow [CuCl_4]^{2-} + H_2O$$

Then when you add the ammonia:
Copper Chloride + Ammonia → Tetraamine Copper + Chlorine
$$[CuCl_4]^{2-} + NH_3 \rightarrow [Cu(NH_3)_4]^{2+} + Cl^-$$

In this experiment it is possible to send the reaction backward by adding more Hydrochloric acid. That's what makes this a reversible reaction. Cool, huh?

The above equations are unbalanced. Can you balance them?

☺ ☻ ☻ EXPERIMENT: Iodine Clock Reaction

This is a great experiment to show reaction rates. You mix two clear liquids and they stay clear until suddenly, poof, you have a dark purple/black solution all at once.

Fabulous Facts

Copper sulfate can be used to make beautifully colored crystals and colored fire. What color do you think they'll end up?

Hydrochloric acid can be used to test rocks for the presence of calcium: if it fizzes there's calcium.

On the Web

Here is a professor showing what happens when copper sulfate and ammonia are combined, part of the Green to Blue experiment:
https://youtu.be/jxoHB_sTkI8

You may need to review what a precipitate is.

Remember to practice balancing equations too.

Additional Layer

A lot of acid and base reactions can be reversed as well. Mix vinegar with baking soda and test with pH papers to see the substance change from acidic to basic and back again as you adjust quantities.

BOSTON TEA PARTY – JAPAN – MORE REACTIONS – FOLK MUSIC

On the Web

There are many different versions of the iodine clock reaction. Those performed in chemistry labs usually use sulfuric acid, which you can obtain for home, but we thought we'd make it easier and cheaper. You can watch the Iodine Clock Reaction on YouTube.
https://youtu.be/KWJpKNQfXWo

Teaching Tip

Not many parents feel comfortable teaching chemistry, but there's help!

Khan Academy and Bozeman Science both have excellent video lectures that cover an entire year of high school chemistry.

We also like *Chemistry: A Self Teaching Guide* and *CK Chemistry* (which is free on Kindle), both on Amazon. Couple these resources with our experiments and you have a high school chemistry program.

Explanation

If you have trouble getting these reactions to work it's probably because the quantities of chemicals aren't quite right. Play with them a bit.

CAUTION: Wear safety goggles when performing this experiment. Dispose of all chemicals in the sink with lots of water.

You need:
- Tincture of Iodine (pharmacy)
- Ascorbic Acid (Vitamin C tablets, pharmacy)
- Hydrogen Peroxide (pharmacy)
- Liquid laundry starch

Procedure:
1. Get three large clear plastic or glass cups or jars. Label them A, B, and C.
2. Mash up 1000 mg of ascorbic acid. Put it into cup A with 60 ml of warm water. Stir well.
3. Put 2 tsp. of liquid A into cup B. Add 1 tsp. of iodine. Stir.
4. In cup C mix 60 ml of warm water, 1 Tbsp. hydrogen peroxide, and ½ tsp. liquid starch.
5. Pour all of liquid B into the cup labeled C. Have someone start a timer the moment you pour the two liquids together. Stir with a clean spoon for about 10 seconds.
6. Let the liquid sit and watch it until it changes color. Record how long it takes to change color.

The iodine and the ascorbic acid are reacting with one another until the ascorbic acid is used up and the iodine "wins." The moment all the ascorbic acid is used up the iodine is free to react with the starch and the solution turns dark.

See how the rate of reaction is affected by temperature changes of the water you begin with, or by the amount of ascorbic acid

Boston Tea Party – Japan – More Reactions – Folk Music

solution (solution A) you use. Time the reaction each time you repeat it and record your results.

☻ **EXPERIMENT: Reversing The Reaction**
Here's another reversible reaction for older students to try out. Zinc, a metal, and iodine, a non-metal, can be combined in this experiment and then the reaction can be reversed with electrolysis.

CAUTION: Use safety equipment, including goggles, gloves, and aprons. The chemicals in this experiment are corrosive and flammable, and this is not an experiment for young kids.

You need:
- zinc powder (Home Science Tools, we'll use zinc powder in unit 3-18 as well)
- iodine solution (Home Science Tools or use iodine solution from a pharmacy; this stains badly, use care)
- ethanol (also called ethyl alcohol or rubbing alcohol and available at pharmacies)
- graduated cylinder
- glass beaker
- test tube and stand
- electrolysis electrodes (from Home Science Tools)
- 6 wire alligator clip leads (Home Science Tools)
- 3- 6 volt batteries
- scientific thermometer (from Home Science Tools)
- distilled water (automotive)

Procedure:
1. Measuring with the graduated cylinder, pour 5 ml ethanol into the test tube.
2. Insert a thermometer and note the temperature.
3. Add 5 drops iodine to the test tube with the alcohol.
4. Stir with the thermometer and note the temperature again.
5. Add 1/8 tsp. zinc powder.
6. Note the temperature again. The temperature should rise. This is an exothermic reaction (giving off heat).
7. The dark brown color of the iodine should have disappeared by the time the reaction is complete. If it has not, add a bit more zinc and stir.
8. Take a few drops of the clear liquid and lay on a glass plate. Allow the liquid to evaporate. You are left with a white crystaline powder. This is zinc iodide.
9. This is the chemical reaction: $Zn + I \longrightarrow Zn+I-$

On the Web

Most reversible reactions settle down to an equilibrium where you cannot see any chemical changes happening unless you add more reactants. But some reactions continue to oscillate indefinitely. These reactions are called chemical clocks.

Here the Professor explains the Belousov – Zhabotinsky reaction, a chemical clock:
https://youtu.be/uWh8reiXq58

Teaching Tip

Sometimes chemical quantities are measured in cc (cubic centimeters) and sometimes in ml.

1 ml = 1 cc

Additional Layer

Zinc is a metal that has been known and described since ancient times. It is mixed with copper to make brass.

Today we know zinc in small amounts is essential for health. Deficiencies of zinc can harm a developing fetus, delay maturation, slow growth, make one more susceptible to infection, and cause diarrhea.

Shellfish and red meats are high in zinc.

Boston Tea Party – Japan – More Reactions – Folk Music

On the Web
This is a video about reaction rates from Mr. Anderson.

https://youtu.be/6mAqX31RRJU

Memorization Station
Including changing the temperature, there are five ways to change the speed in a reaction:

> temperature
> concentration
> surface area
> physical state
> catalysts

Watch this video for an excellent and entertaining explanation on how to change reaction rates.

https://youtu.be/OttRV5ykP7A

Then commit these five methods to memory.

Additional Layer
Besides the five factors above that affect the speed of a reaction, there is one more: light. Some reactions are sped up if the energy from light enters the system giving the molecules more energy to move. An example is the degrading of plastic. This is bad on your greenhouse cover and good for plastic waste.

Now to reverse the reaction, also called decomposing:

1. After you've allowed the solution to sit, pour off the clear liquid into a beaker, leaving any residue at the bottom of the test tube.
2. Add 20 ml of distilled water.
3. Place electrolysis electrodes into the beaker
4. Hook the alligator clips, negative to one side and positive to the other side of the electrode, then hook up each of your batteries in order, making a complete circuit. Be sure to hook negative to positive and so on.
5. Once you have a complete circuit, electrons will begin to flow through the electrodes and into the water. The negative side of the electrode will attract positively charged elements and the positive side will attract negatively charged particles. The zinc iodide will be pulled back apart into its pieces.
6. A brownish substance should form around the positive electrode. This is the negatively charged iodine. The zinc will be forming around the negatively charged electrode.
7. After a few minutes, break the circuit and remove the electrodes from the water. Rinse them off under tap water. A shiny zinc coating should have formed over the end of one electrode.
8. You can test it by dipping the end of the electrode in a little vinegar. The zinc will react and release a colorless gas, hydrogen.

Discussion questions:
- What are the chemical symbols of iodine and zinc? (I and Zn)
- Where are they located on the periodic table?
- Are zinc and iodine metals or non-metals? (Zn is a metal and I is a non-metal)
- Write the chemical equation that is happening in this experiment. (see above)
- Are there equal amounts of Zn and I reacting in this experiment? (yes, it is a one to one ratio)
- What kind of bond are the iodine and zinc forming? (an ionic bond, they are attracted to each other by their charges)
- The reaction gives off heat. What is it called when a reaction gives off heat? (exothermic)
- What does it mean that a reaction is reversible? (You can return to the components you began with)
- What did we have to do to get the zinc and the iodine back out of solution? (electrolysis)
- Why was the zinc attracted to one electrode while the iodine was attracted to the other? (they are charged ionic particles, which are attracted by their opposite charges. The charge in

the electrodes was greater than the strength of the ionic bonds, so the elements were attracted to the electrodes.)

😊 😊 😊 EXPERIMENT: Reaction Rates

Certain conditions can make a chemical reaction happen faster or slower. One way to change the speed of a reaction is to change the temperature.

Try this:
1. Prepare two glasses, one filled with very hot tap water and one filled with ice water.
2. Break two glow sticks, shake them and observe.
3. Place one stick in the cold water and one in the hot.

Which glow stick is brighter? Let them sit overnight. Which glow stick lasts longer?

The heat in the hot water sped up the reaction of the chemicals. The cold water slowed the reaction, making the stick less bright, but also allowing it to last longer.

😊 😊 😊 EXPERIMENT: Plop Plop, Fizz Fizz!

1. Fill a test tube or small jar half full of cool tap water.
2. Place a thermometer in the water and record the temperature before the reaction and during the reaction.
3. Break four Alka-Seltzer tablets in half and drop all the pieces in the water at once. Time the reaction from when you drop it in until it stops.

Additional Layer

It is thought that in order for molecules to react they must collide, or actually physically touch. This is called collision theory.

Here is an explanation of collision theory from Khan Academy: https://youtu.be/1iAxhc6EflI

Additional Layer

An endothermic reaction takes heat from the surroundings and uses it as energy. The endothermic reaction will drop in temperature during the reaction.

An exothermic reaction gives heat off to the surroundings as it loses energy. It will rise in temperature during the reaction.

Mr. Anderson explains: https://youtu.be/L-G7pLufXA0

More Experiments

Since you bought Alka Seltzer for an experiment already you might as well do some more. Here are some experiment ideas from Bayer, the maker of Alka Seltzer: http://www.alkaseltzer.com/as/student_experiment.html.

Boston Tea Party – Japan – More Reactions – Folk Music

From the Books

The concepts from this unit are taught in chapter 12 of *Chemistry: A Self-Teaching Guide* by Clifford C. Houk and Richard Post.

And at Khan Academy:
https://www.khanacademy.org/science/chemistry/chemical-equilibrium
https://www.khanacademy.org/science/chemistry/chem-kinetics

Writer's Workshop

Write a scene where the hero has to either slow down or speed up a reaction rate to save the day. Slow a heart or bleeding? Speed an exothermic reaction to produce heat? Speed burning to explosion?

Famous Folks

Humphry Davy was a chemist from Cornwall in Wales. He discovered elemental chlorine and elemental iodine.

This reaction is endothermic, the chemical reaction pulls heat from the surroundings and so it cools the water.

Repeat the reaction, but this time start with hot water. How does the temperature of the water affect the rate of reaction?

Repeat the experiment again, but this time use pressure to affect the rate of reaction.
1. Put a stopper in the test tube or a lid on the jar right after dropping the tablets into the water. You'll have to let off a little gas from time to time or you'll break your glassware.
2. Eventually the reaction will stop as the pressure trying to get out of liquid and the pressure pushing down on the liquid are equal. You should still have some solid Alka Seltzer bits in the water. Record the time of the reaction to reach equilibrium under pressure.
3. Let the lid off and watch the reaction start again.

☺ ☺ ☺ **EXPERIMENT: Mechanical Reaction Rate**
In the above experiments we learned that temperature and pressure can affect reactions rates, but so can mechanical means, like stirring.

Procedure:
1. Put 100 ml (½ c.) room temperature water into a beaker or glass jar.
2. Add ½ tsp. baking soda and 40 ml (2.5 Tablespoons) vinegar. Let it sit; do not stir. Record the reaction time until the reaction stops.

Boston Tea Party – Japan – More Reactions – Folk Music

3. Repeat the experiment, but this time stir the solution the entire time and record how long it takes for the reaction to complete.

😊 ☺ **EXPERIMENT: Mentos Volcano**

Put your hand over your heart and repeat after me: Explosions are fun! This is an outdoor activity as it will make a big mess.

You need:
- Mentos candy
- Diet Coke
- Index card
- Paper

Procedure:
1. Remove your Mentos from the package and roll them into a piece of paper in a single stack.
2. Loosen the cap from your soda bottle and shake it a little.
3. Place an index card over the end of the paper tube of Mentos to keep the candies from falling out.
4. Take the cap off your bottle and invert the roll of candies onto the top of the bottle, with the index card on bottom to keep the candies from falling into the bottle.
5. Slide the index card out in one smooth motion so the candy falls neatly into the bottle and then take cover!

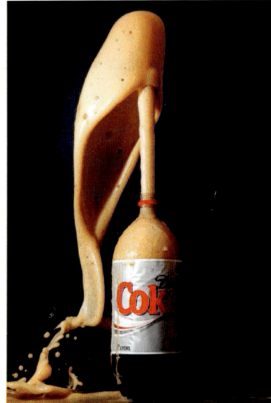
Photo by Michael Murphy, CC license, Wikimedia.

You will soon have a fountain of soda arcing gracefully through the sky.

The soda is full of carbon dioxide gas which wants to get out of the soda and into the air. This happens fairly slowly under normal conditions, but the gelatin and gum arabic from the dissolving Mentos breaks the surface tension and increases the reaction speed, making all the carbon dioxide exit post haste, yet another catalyst, though instead of a chemical catalyst this one is a physical catalyst. Also note the rate of reaction (carbon dioxide

Famous Folks

Alfred Nobel was a Swedish chemist. He invented dynamite which made him extremely wealthy. With his money he established a fund to reward scientists for great discoveries, the Nobel Prizes.

Additional Layer

Mentos candy was created in the Netherlands by Jim Mentos in 1948. Think up your own spectacularly selling candy. Would it be fruity or chocolaty? Would it be chewy or crunchy? Would it be smooth or chunky? Would it be sweet or sour?

On the Web

Have your middle grades kids read this page and then click on the link for the quiz near the bottom: http://www.chem4kids.com/files/react_rates.html.

BOSTON TEA PARTY – JAPAN – MORE REACTIONS – FOLK MUSIC

Additional Layer
All living things have the enzyme catalase in their bodies. When cells do their thing they produce hydrogen peroxide, which is toxic (some people think a lack of catalase makes our hair turn gray too). The catalase changes the hydrogen peroxide into harmless oxygen and water.

Additional Layer

Humans are missing the enzyme that forms vitamin C, which is why sailors used to get scurvy when they were out at sea away from fresh foods. Most animals and plants have the vitamin C enzyme, so eating almost anything raw will supply Vitamin C.

Fabulous Facts
Enzymes are used for millions of processes in your body every day like digestion, DNA copying, and changing glucose into body energy.

leaving the liquid and reforming a gas), before and after the Mentos are added.

☺ ☺ ☺ EXPERIMENT: Enzymes
Enzymes are catalysts that can be found in living things. Enzymes help the organism to break down food and make proteins.

Try this:
1. Get two test tubes and pour 2 Tbsp. of hydrogen peroxide into each one.
2. Put a drop of dish soap into each tube as well (this is purely for dramatic effect as the gas given off in the experiment will make the bubbles foam up.)
3. Drop diced raw liver into one test tube and diced raw potato into the other.

Which one reacts more violently and produces more bubbles? The liver has more of the enzyme catalase than the potato does.

Here is the reaction:
$$H_2O_2 + \text{catalase} \rightarrow H_2O + O_2$$
hydrogen peroxide + catalase →water + oxygen

The catalase isn't used up in the experiment, catalysts never are, they just make the reaction happen or happen faster.

The Arts: Folk Music

Folk music includes songs and tunes that are traditional, usually from previous generations, and authored anonymously. They are passed down through generations and can often be changed over time or from place to place. For example, a popular folk song in England might get new lyrics in America. A tune used for one song in France might be used for another one in Argentina.

Folk music is written by regular people – folks. It is also written for regular people – folks. Since it is the music of the common people it can often be a window into the culture of the people. You can learn what is important to them, which historical events or heroes remain in their memory, and something about their attitudes toward fun and leisure.

The Turning of the Tune, Currier and Ives lithograph, 1870

☺ ☺ ☺ EXPLORATION: World Music

Another name for folk music is world music, because it is music that represents so many areas and cultures of the world. Listen to samples of folk music from around the world and try to identify where they are from. You can use this YouTube video: https://youtu.be/pHa1S3_kxGA. Notice that the location shows on the screen at the beginning of each music clip. Don't peek! Have the kids try to guess the place before finding out. Folk music from different areas has distinctive sounds, much more so than classical music. Once you've found out where it is from,

---

Teaching Tip

A book of nursery rhymes is a great companion to your study of folk music. The rhymes are poems and folk songs for children.

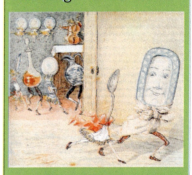

On the Web

This site has a collection of folk music from all around the world (in the form of You Tube Videos). Watch and listen to the different sounds of folk music. What do you learn about the cultures?

http://kidsmusiccorner.co.uk/types/folk-music/

Expedition

See if there is a folk music festival happening near where you live. These are most common in the summer months. Attend if you can.

BOSTON TEA PARTY – JAPAN – MORE REACTIONS – FOLK MUSIC

Writer's Workshop

A ballad is a song that tells a story. The most famous are those about John Henry and Casey Jones. Read those, then think of a personal story from your life that you could put into a song. Write song lyrics to tell the story. If you haven't written music before, the easiest way is to choose an already familiar tune and just write the words to the tune you already know well.

The famous Casey Jones on a postage stamp.

Additional Layer

Ring Around the Rosie was another choreographed dance meant to help young beaus dance appropriately in a day when physical contact between young men and women was frowned upon.

Additional Layer

"Lou" in the title of Skip to my Lou comes from the Scottish word "loo," meaning love.

color that area on the map from the printables section. Note that a few of the places have more than one song clip, but you'll only color one place on the map for them. When you've listened to all the songs, discuss how the music was alike and different. If you'd like to listen to more, there are more YouTube videos in the same series with more folk song samples from around the world.

☺ ☻ **EXPLORATION: Singing Folk Songs**

Pick one of the folk songs from this page: http://www.songsforteaching.com/folk/. Teach your kids to sing it. Have them perform it for an audience; Grandma or the neighbors will work just fine. Many of the songs are lots of fun. While you're doing this unit, sing many of these songs over and over and you'll all learn them. Here are a few we really love:
- The Bear Went Over the Mountain
- BINGO
- She'll Be Comin' Round the Mountain
- The Ants Go Marching
- Going on a Bear Hunt
- Here We Go Round the Mulberry Bush
- Yankee Doodle
- When the Saints Go Marching In
- Apples and Bananas
- Alice the Camel
- Down By The Bay

☺ ☻ ☻ **EXPLORATION: Song and Dance**

Learn Skip to My Lou and make up a dance that goes with it. http://freesongsforkids.com/audios/skip-my-lou. There have been square dances, Hip Hop dances, preschool dances, and even a Just Dance video game routine choreographed to this song. It started off as a square dance that was made in the early America when it was thought that close dancing and contact between young men and women was immoral. They choreographed square dances so they could get together and dance without the objectionable closeness and one on one contact of dancing.

In the traditional Skip To My Lou, a ring of couples skip around in a circle. One boy in the center sings "Lost my partner, what'll I do? I'll get another one just like you," and then he grabs a partner's hand. Her former partner now goes to the middle and begins the game again. They dance around and around, always singing and switching partners. If you've never been to a square dance, you might try to find a group who meets in your area. It's lots of fun and they generally love teaching it to new people. You'll pick it up in no time.

BOSTON TEA PARTY – JAPAN – MORE REACTIONS – FOLK MUSIC

☺ ☻ **EXPLORATION: Song Styles**
One of the fun things about folk music is that it changes all the time. People sing the same songs in new styles and new ways. Let's try out some song styles using the song Dry Bones:
   http://freesongsforkids.com/audios/dry-bones

First, listen to and learn the song. Make up your own motions to go with the song. Now try singing it with different styles. Here are a few ideas to get you started:
- surfer style
- cowboy style
- fairy tale style
- granny style
- scary monster style
- hula dancer style
- monster truck driver style
- Hip Hop dancer style
- pirate style

☺ ☻ **EXPLORATION: The Origin of Song**
Sometimes we know the origins and stories of folk songs and sometimes we don't. There are certainly some fascinating stories to uncover though.

Yankee Doodle was a pre-Revolutionary War song that both the Brits and American colonists used to poke fun at the other. The Brits used it to insinuate that the American "Yankee" soldiers were foolish and feminine, while the Americans took the insult and turned it into a patriotic tribute to snub the British. New verses were added based on incidents and battles that arose over their years of conflict.

Choose some folk songs to research and see if you can find out what events spurred them on. Make a small booklet called "The Origins of Folk Songs." At the top of each page write the song title, then write about where it came from and the interesting events surrounding it.

Additional Layer

We Shall Overcome became an anthem of the Civil Rights Movement. Dr. Martin Luther King quoted it in his final speech and, just a few days later, over fifty thousand people sang it together at his funeral. Songs can be powerful unifying tools, and folk music has been used for accomplishing a lot of good in the world.

On The Web
This video tells a bit about the history of folk music in America:
http://www.zaneeducation.com/Videos/Music/History_Of_Music/American_Folk_Music/The_Roots_of_American_Folk_Music.php

Additional Layer
Harmonicas, banjos, fiddles, and accordions are all folk instruments.

Boston Tea Party – Japan – More Reactions – Folk Music

Additional Layer
In the United States, beginning in the 1940's, there was a huge revival of folk music when professional musicians began to sing traditional folk songs. They created a new commercialized version of folk style.

Additional Layer

Woody Guthrie was a famous folk singer who lived through the Great Depression and the Dust Bowl, then wrote songs about poverty, ecology, and unions in the United States.

Additional Layer
Cajun, Blues, and Country music genres all stemmed from folk music originally. They each had ethnic roots and were influenced by the geography and culture of the folks from their areas.

🙂🙂🙂 EXPLORATION: Five Little Monkeys
Some folk music has been made into other art forms. One of our favorite children's books is based on the lyrics of the folk song, Five Little Monkeys. It's called *Five Little Monkeys Jumping On The Bed* by Eileen Christelow.

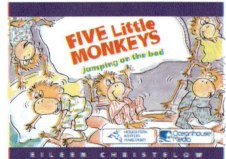

Choose your own folk song and use the lyrics from it to make a picture book. Design a terrific cover, write the words in your best handwriting, and illustrate it colorfully. Share it with someone.

🙂🙂🙂 EXPLORATION: Musical Mural
Choose a folk song to use as inspiration for a mural. Get a large poster or roll of butcher paper to hang on the wall. Listen to the song and have everyone participate in making a mural of the song using markers, crayons, paint, colorful paper, fabric scraps, ribbons, and other art supplies. Here are some suggested songs:
- Jenny Jenkins
- The Green Grass Grew All Around
- A Sailor Went To Sea
- Animal Fair
- Boom, Boom, Ain't It Great To Be Crazy

🙂🙂 EXPLORATION: Expressions of History
Folk music isn't all simple children's songs. Often historical events are at the root of folk music. Music has been used to encourage collective action or right social or societal wrongs. For example, Negro spirituals encouraged Christian morals and ideals while also lamenting the mistreatment of an entire group of people. Folk music was also used to collectively inspire a group of people to work hard and well together, like the men working on the railroad lines.

Choose one of these events and write a five paragraph essay about how music was used to explore the historical issues of the day in the United States.
- Slavery of African-Americans – negro spirituals
- Student Movements of the 1960's – protest songs
- Texas-Mexicans – the Corrido
- Labor union organizers – Union songs
- Cowboys – Cowboy ballads
- Development of the Railroad – Railroad songs
- Civil War – Gospel music

BOSTON TEA PARTY – JAPAN – MORE REACTIONS – FOLK MUSIC

☺ ☺ ☻ **EXPEDITION: Sing Along**

Have a sing along with a group of neighbors around campfire or in the living room. Serve a treat like s'mores or popcorn. If anyone plays the guitar, harmonica, fiddle, or another portable instrument you could incorporate that as well. Most people will know the tunes and lyrics, but song sheets would be nice. If you have discovered any of the interesting origins of the tunes you are singing, you could also use this as an opportunity to tell about them.

☺ ☺ ☻ **EXPLORATION: Instrumental**

Learn to play a folk song on a recorder or on a glockenspiel. This site has some free sheet music:
http://www.8notes.com/all/childrens/sheet_music/

☺ ☻ **EXPLORATION: Technology and Folk Music**

Have a discussion about the effects of technology on folk music. Here are some discussion questions to help you get started:
- What impact do you think technology has had on music in the past twenty years? What impact does it have on folk music in particular?
- Has the globalization of music caused us to change or adapt our styles in new ways?
- Do you know of any songs or singers from a country other than your own? Would this be possible without our technology?
- Are there any drawbacks to having musical technology? Have we lost anything because of it? Have musicians lost anything because of it?
- Are there any advantages to having musical technology? Does it bring the world closer together or drive us further apart?
- How do you think technology has impacted the way we tell our cultural stories through song throughout the world?

Writer's Workshop

The Didgeridoo is a famous folk instrument from Australia. The bagpipes are one from Scotland. Fiddles and accordians are used in Denmark. The cavaquinho is a Portuguese folk instrument.

Choose any country in the world and do some research into what instruments and traditional music comes from the folks in that country.

Write about it.

Folk Instruments, Public Domain

Coming up next . . .

Unit 3-18

Founding Fathers
Iran – Compounds
Rococo

Boston Tea Party – Japan – More Reactions – Folk Music

My Ideas For This Unit:

Title: _____   Topic: _____

_____
_____
_____
_____
_____
_____
_____
_____
_____

Title: _____   Topic: _____

_____
_____
_____
_____
_____
_____
_____
_____
_____

Title: _____   Topic: _____

_____
_____
_____
_____
_____
_____
_____
_____
_____

Boston Tea Party – Japan – More Reactions – Folk Music

My Ideas For This Unit:

Title: _____   Topic: _____

_____
_____
_____
_____
_____
_____
_____
_____
_____

Title: _____   Topic: _____

_____
_____
_____
_____
_____
_____
_____
_____
_____

Title: _____   Topic: _____

_____
_____
_____
_____
_____
_____
_____
_____
_____

Boston Tea Party

In December of 1773 men in Boston dressed as Indians to disguise themselves, boarded ships in Boston Harbor, and destroyed the entire cargo of tea on those ships. They were protesting unfair laws by their government back in Britain including taxes on tea and special rules that gave the British East India Company a trade advantage.

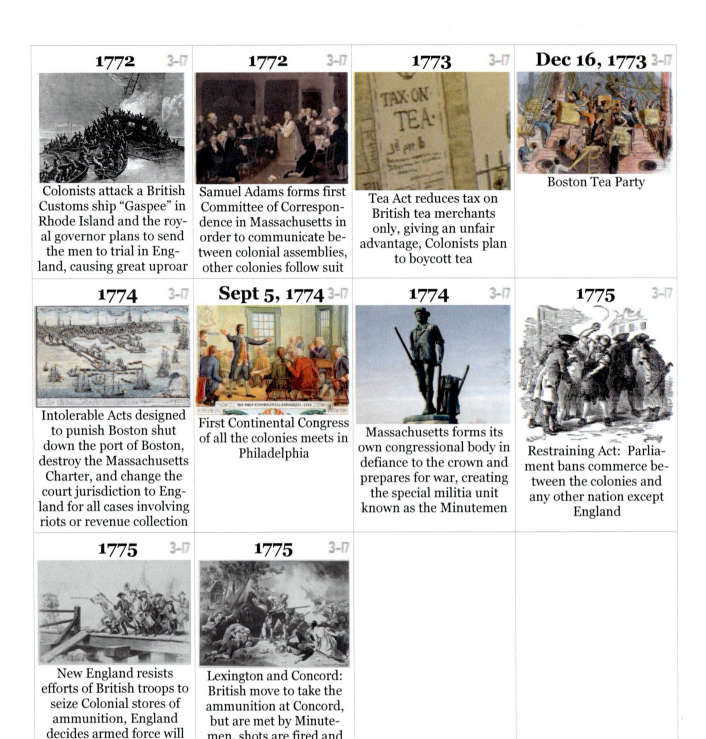

North America at the Close of the French and Indian War

- British land
- Newly gained British territory
- Spanish land
- Newly gained Spanish territory

Layers of Learning

Faneuil Hall

Cut out the craft all around the outside lines. Color the Hall. It was built of red bricks with white painted trim. Turn the paper over and write some of the things that were said or done here and the names of some of the famous people who met here. Then fold along the solid lines to make the walls and roof. Glue the walls and roof together with the flaps.

Layers of Learning

Boston Tea Party Diorama Figures

Layers of Learning

Japan

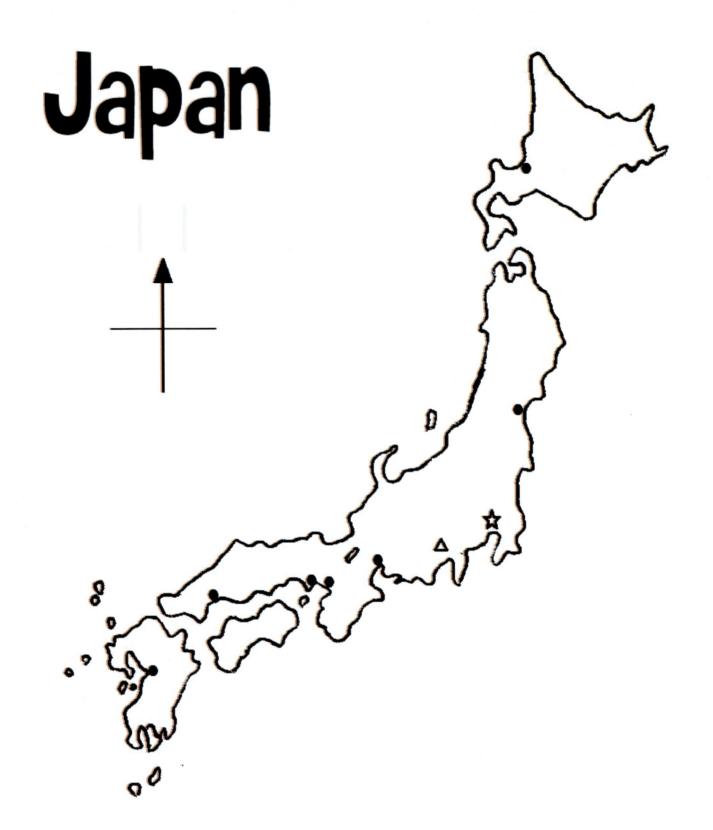

Layers of Learning

Kokeshi Dolls

Kimono Report

Layers of Learning

Folk Music From Around The World

Scotland
Portugal
Spain
Italy
Japan
China
Iran
Middle East
Egypt
India
North Africa
Sub-Saharan Africa
United States
Mexico
Cuba
Peru
Brazil
Argentina

Layers of Learning

About the Authors

Karen & Michelle . . .
Mothers, sisters, teachers, women who are passionate
about educating kids.
We are dedicated to lifelong learning.

Karen, a mother of four, who has homeschooled her kids for more than eight years with her husband, Bob, has a bachelor's degree in child development with an emphasis in education. She lives in Idaho, gardens, teaches piano, and plays an excruciating number of board games with her kids. Karen is our resident arts expert and English guru {most necessary as Michelle regularly and carelessly mangles the English language and occasionally steps over the bounds of polite society}.

Michelle and her husband, Cameron, have homeschooled their six boys for more than a decade. Michelle earned a bachelors in biology, making her the resident science expert, though she is mocked by her friends for being the *Botanist with the Black Thumb of Death*. She also is the go-to for history and government. She believes in staying up late, hot chocolate, and a no whining policy. We both pitch in on geography, in case you were wondering, and are on a continual quest for knowledge.

*Visit our constantly updated blog for tons of free ideas,
free printables, and more cool stuff for sale:*
www.Layers-of-Learning.com